PRIMARY CLASSIC READ

Sleeping Beauty

Adapted for ELT by Jennifer Heath

NEW EDITIONS
English Language Teaching

Sleeping Beauty

Adapted for ELT by Jennifer Heath

For permission to use material from this
text or product, submit a request online at
http://www.thomsonrights.com

Any additional questions about
permissions can be submitted by email to
thomsonrights@thomson.com

ISBN-13: 978-960-403-393-5
ISBN-10: 960-403-393-X

Printed in Croatia.
2 3 4 5 6 7 8 9 10   11 10 09 08 07

For more information contact Thomson Heinle,
High Holborn House, 50/51 Bedford Row, London WC1R 4LR United Kingdom,
or you can visit our Internet site at elt.thomson.com

Acknowledgments
Recording and production at GFS-PRO Studio by George Flamouridis
Original Spanish title: La Bella Durmiente
Original Edition © Parramon Ediciones SA, Barcelona, España

De le Ann pare Magdalene, Cuero, 2014

Contents

One day, a good King and his beautiful Queen have a baby. They are very happy.

'Let's have a party,' says the King.

The King and Queen invite their friends to the party. They also invite seven good fairies.

Today is the party! Everybody gives a present to the baby princess. The fairies also give presents. Their presents are very special.

'You will be beautiful,' says the first fairy.
'You will be clever,' says the second fairy.
'You will be kind,' says the third fairy.
'You will sing,' says the fourth fairy.
'You will dance,' says the fifth fairy.
'You will always be happy,' says the sixth fairy.

Suddenly, somebody knocks on the palace door.

It's a bad fairy. She is very ugly. Everybody is afraid of her. The bad fairy is angry because the King didn't ask her to come to the party.

'I want to give the princess my present,' says the bad fairy. She points to the baby princess and she says, 'When she's sixteen, she'll cut her finger on a spinning wheel and die!'

The bad fairy laughs and leaves.

Everybody is very sad. But the seventh fairy can help.

'Don't worry. Here's my present. The princess won't die. She will sleep for one hundred years,' she says. 'Then a prince will kiss her and she will wake up.'

The King and Queen are afraid. The King wants to hide all the spinning wheels. He sends a messenger to the town.

'Hide your spinning wheels. We must save the princess,' says the messenger.

The princess is a young woman now. She's beautiful, clever and kind. She can sing and dance. She's always happy. But she's also very curious.

Today is her birthday. She's sixteen.

The princess is walking in the palace. She sees some stairs. Suddenly, she hears a noise. The princess is curious and she goes up the stairs.

The stairs go up a tower. There is a room at the top of the tower. The princess opens the door. She sees an ugly woman. It's the bad fairy!

'Hello. What are you doing?' asks the princess.

'I'm spinning. Do you want to try?' says the bad fairy.

'Yes, I do,' says the princess.

The princess sits down at the spinning wheel. Suddenly, she cuts her finger and she falls asleep!

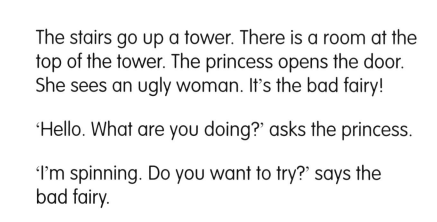

The King and Queen find the princess. They put her in her bed. They remember the bad fairy's words. The King and Queen are crying.

'We mustn't cry,' says the King. 'Remember the seventh fairy's present. Our beautiful daughter won't die. She's sleeping. She will sleep for one hundred years.'

Everybody in the kingdom is sad. The men and women aren't singing or dancing. The children aren't playing. They want to see the princess again.

One day, the King goes to the good fairy. He wants her help.

'I can't wake up the princess,' says the good fairy. 'But I can help you.'

The good fairy goes to the top of a hill. She looks at the kingdom and she waves her magic wand.

Suddenly, everybody in the kingdom falls asleep. The King and Queen fall asleep. The men and the women fall asleep. The children fall asleep. The animals fall asleep.

The good fairy waves her magic wand again.
Suddenly, a forest grows around the kingdom.
The trees are very tall and they hide the kingdom.
For one hundred years, nobody goes there.

One hundred years later, a prince is riding his horse. He sees the forest. He can see towers behind the trees.

'What's that in the forest?' he asks a farmer.

'There is a kingdom in the forest. Everybody in the kingdom is sleeping,' says the farmer.

The farmer tells the prince the story about the bad fairy and the beautiful princess.

'We call the princess Sleeping Beauty,' says the farmer.
'One day, a prince will kiss her and she will wake up.'

The prince is curious. He wants to see Sleeping Beauty.

The prince goes into the forest. He cuts the trees with his sword. He cuts and cuts. He's very tired.

The good fairy is hiding in the forest. She helps the prince. She waves her magic wand and the trees move. Now the prince can find the kingdom.

The prince goes into the palace. It's very quiet! The people and the animals are sleeping.

The prince is looking for Sleeping Beauty. He sees some stairs. He goes up the stairs and he finds her in the tallest tower.

Sleeping Beauty is sleeping on her bed. She's very beautiful. The prince falls in love with her!

The prince kisses Sleeping Beauty. Suddenly, she wakes up! She opens her eyes. She sees the prince and she smiles. The princess falls in love with the prince.

'Thank you, handsome prince,' she says.

Everybody in the kingdom wakes up. The King and Queen wake up. The men and women wake up. The children wake up. The animals wake up.

The prince and princess marry. Everybody in the kingdom is happy again.

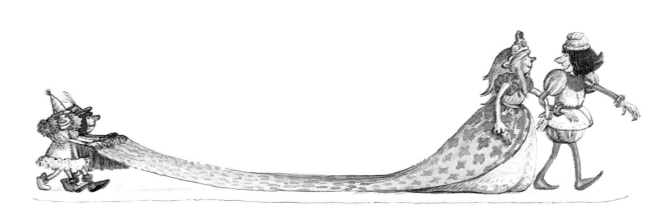

Activities

A Match.

a

d

1 baby

2 stairs

3 spinning wheel

4 tower

5 magic wand

6 present

b

c

e

f

B Tick (✓) true or false.

	T	F
1 The King and Queen invite their friends to the party.		
2 The bad fairy isn't ugly.		
3 The King sends a fairy to the town.		
4 The princess is curious.		
5 The prince kisses Sleeping Beauty.		
6 The animals don't wake up.		

finger   forest   hundred   kingdom
messenger   prince   seven   sword

1   The King and Queen invite .... good fairies to the party.

2   'We must save the princess,' says the ....

3   The princess cuts her .... and she falls asleep!

4   The princess will sleep for one .... years.

5   Everybody in the .... falls asleep.

6   A .... grows around the kingdom.

7   The prince cuts the trees with his ....

8   The princess falls in love with the ....

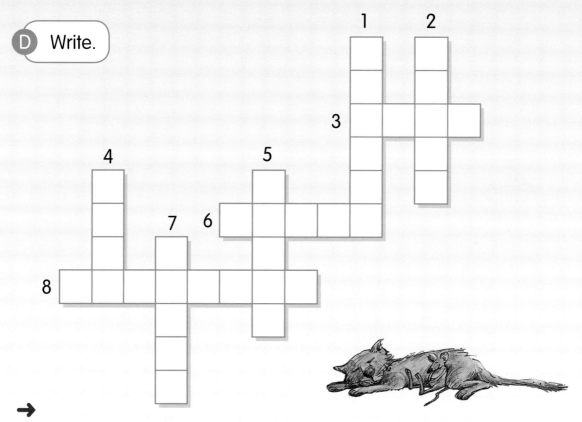

→
3 The princess can ..... and dance.
6 Suddenly, everybody in the kingdom ..... asleep.
8 The King and Queen ..... the bad fairy's words.

↓
1 The prince ..... Sleeping Beauty.
2 The prince ..... Sleeping Beauty in the tallest tower.
4 The trees ..... the kingdom.
5 The good fairy ..... her magic wand.
7 The good fairy ..... the prince.

cry   curious   farmer   handsome
horse   kiss   laugh
palace   sixteen   sleep

```
S  L  K  P  C  R  Y  O  P
L  S  I  X  T  E  E  N  A
A  L  S  F  C  C  U  V  L
J  E  S  G  U  H  A  N  A
L  E  F  A  R  M  E  R  C
A  P  O  F  I  G  B  J  E
U  D  S  H  O  R  S  E  T
G  L  T  D  U  C  F  O  N
H  A  N  D  S  O  M  E  V
```

33

F Colour.

Picture Glossary

cry	fairy	farmer	forest
kingdom	laugh	magic wand	messenger
present	prince	sleep	spinning wheel
stairs	sword	tower	ugly